Calvin and Hobbes

by Bill Watterson

A TRUMPET CLUB SPECIAL EDITION

Published by The Trumpet Club
666 Fifth Avenue, New York, New York 10103

Calvin and Hobbes® is syndicated internationally by Universal
Press Syndicate.

Copyright © 1987 by Bill Watterson

ISBN 0-440-84481-9

This edition published by arrangement with Andrews and
McMeel, a Universal Press Syndicate Company
Printed in the United States of America
January 1992

10 9 8 7 6 5 4 3 2 1
CUS

Foreword

There are few wellsprings of humor more consistently reliable than the mind of a child. Most cartoonists, being childlike, recognize this, but when they set out to capture the hurly-burly of the very young, they almost always cheat, shamelessly creating not recognizable children, but highly annoying, wisecracking, miniature adults. Chalk it up to either indolence or defective recall, but most people who write comic dialogue for minors (up to and including the perpetrators of the Cosby "kids") demonstrate surprisingly little feel for — or faith in — the original source material, that is, childhood, in all its unfettered and winsome glory.

It is in this respect that Bill Watterson has proved as unusual as his feckless creations, Calvin and Hobbes. Watterson is the reporter who's gotten it right; childhood as it actually *is*, with its constantly shifting frames of reference. Anyone who's done time with a small child knows that reality can be highly situational. The utterance which an adult knows to be a "lie" may well reflect a child's deepest conviction, at least at the moment it pops out. Fantasy is so accessible, and it is joined with such force and frequency, that resentful parents like Calvin's assume they are being manipulated, when the truth is far more frightening: they don't even exist. The child is both king and keeper of this realm, and he can be very choosey about the company he keeps.

Of course, this exclusivity only provokes many grown-ups into trying to regain the serendipity of youth for themselves, to, in effect, retrieve the irretrievable. A desperate few do things that later land them in the Betty Ford Center.

The rest of us, more sensibly, read Calvin and Hobbes.

— GARRY TRUDEAU

TO MELISSA

OUTRAGE! WHY SHOULD I GO TO BED? I'M NOT TIRED! IT'S ONLY 7:30! THIS IS TYRANNY! I'M!

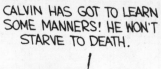

OUR HERO, THE VALIANT SPACEMAN SPIFF, IS MAROONED ON A STRANGE WORLD...

I'LL SET MY MERTILIZER ON "DEEP FAT FRY."

CALVIN! YOU'RE NOT PAYING ATTENTION!

..WE JOIN SPACEMAN SPIFF ON THE DISTANT PLANET ZORG...

GRONK! ARGH!

ZOUNDS!

TRAPPED BY A HIDEOUS GRAKNIL, SPIFF DRAWS HIS TRUSTY ATOMIC NAPALM NEUTRALIZER!

CHEW ELECTRIC DEATH, SNARLING CUR!

BUT THE WEAPON IS USELESS! SPIFF IS DOOMED!!

OUR HERO MAKES A BREAK, AND DUCKS INTO A NEARBY CAVE!

WEEOOO! WHAT'S THAT AWFUL SMELL?

EEP!

TEACHERS LOUNGE

WHO WAS THAT?

BEATS ME, FRED.

SLAM!

WATTERSON

14

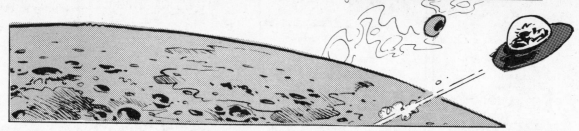

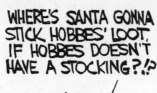

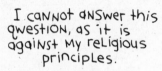

37

HI, DAD. IT'S ME, CALVIN!

HOW'S WORK GOING? ...UH HUH... PRETTY DAY OUT, ISN'T IT? ... YEP.....

ARE YOU BRINGING ME HOME ANY PRESENTS TONIGHT? ...NO? WELL, JUST THOUGHT I'D ASK...

LISTEN, I SUPPOSE YOU'RE WONDERING WHY I CALLED...

DAD, YOUR POLLS TOOK A BIG DIVE THIS WEEK.

YOUR "OVERALL DAD PERFORMANCE" RATING WAS ESPECIALLY LOW.

SEE? RIGHT ABOUT YESTERDAY YOUR POPULARITY WENT DOWN THE TUBES.

CALVIN, YOU DIDN'T GET DESSERT YESTERDAY BECAUSE YOU FLOODED THE HOUSE!!

I'D SUGGEST A NEW LINE OF WORK, "DAD"...

THE GIANT SLIMY OCTOPUS OOZES ACROSS THE BEACH.

HIS HIDEOUS PRESENCE TERRORIZES THE SLEEPY WATERFRONT COMMUNITY.

WITH A SUCKER-COVERED TENTACLE, HE GRABS AN UNSUSPECTING TOURIST.

A MUFFLED SCREAM LINGERS IN THE SALTY AIR!

DID YOU WANT SOMETHING, CALVIN?

ACK ICK IG

WHAT SHOULD WE HAVE DAD READ US TONIGHT?

..SO IN THE NEXT PANEL, SUPERTOAD GOES "PLOOIE", AND...

" 'MY, WHAT BIG TEETH YOU HAVE!' SAID LITTLE RED RIDING HOOD. 'THE BETTER TO EAT YOU WITH!' SAID THE WOLF..."

TIGER.

"..SAID THE TIGER, AND HE POUNCED ON LITTLE RED RIDING HOOD."

"JUST THEN A HUNTER CAME BY, AND WHEN HE SAW THE WOLF..."

TIGER.

"..WHEN HE SAW THE TIGER, HE PICKED UP HIS GUN AND..."

"AND?

"..AND IT WAS TOO LATE. THE TIGER ATE THEM BOTH AND HE LIVED HAPPILY EVER AFTER. THE END."

GOOD STORY, DAD! THANKS!

SNIFF I ALWAYS CRY AT HAPPY ENDINGS.

WATTERSON

"A BUSHEL IS A UNIT OF WEIGHT EQUAL TO FOUR PECKS."

WHAT'S A PECK?

A QUICK SMOOCH.

YOU KNOW, I DON'T UNDERSTAND MATH AT ALL.

MOM, CAN I HAVE SOME MONEY SO HOBBES AND I CAN GO TO A MOVIE?

WHAT MOVIE?

"THE CUISINART MURDERER OF CENTRAL HIGH!"

I REALLY THINK THERE ARE MORE CONSTRUCTIVE WAYS YOU COULD SPEND YOUR AFTERNOON, CALVIN.

WHAT DID SHE SAY?

OH, SHE WENT OFF ON ONE OF HER IRRELEVANT TANGENTS AGAIN.

DO YOU BELIEVE OUR DESTINIES ARE CONTROLLED BY THE STARS?

NO, I THINK WE CAN DO WHATEVER WE WANT WITH OUR LIVES.

NOT TO HEAR MOM AND DAD TELL IT.

WAKE UP, CALVIN. IT'S TIME FOR SCHOOL.

I'M NOT GOING TO SCHOOL ANYMORE.

YOU HAVE TO. IT'S THE LAW.

WHAT ABOUT HOBBES? WHY DOESN'T *HE* HAVE TO GO TO SCHOOL?

HE'S A TIGER. GET UP.

WHAT'S BEING A TIGER GOT TO DO WITH IT?

TIGERS WRECK THE GRADE CURVE.

DO YOU THINK IT'S BETTER TO LIVE IN STUPEFYING SECURITY...

...OR TO TAKE RISKS AND LIVE LIFE ON THE EDGE?

I THINK IT'S BETTER TO ACCEPT DANGER AND LIVE TO THE FULLEST!

I TAKE IT BY YOUR SILENCE THAT YOU AGREE...

I'M MAKING SUSIE DERKINS A VALENTINE.

SHE'S A CUTIE, ALL RIGHT.

SEE, I MADE A BIG RED HEART.

NOW I'M PUTTING LACE AROUND IT.

THAT'S VERY SWEET. I'M SURE SHE'LL LIKE IT.

Susie, I hate you. Drop dead. Calvin

HEY, CALVIN! ARE WE NEAR A SLAUGHTERHOUSE, OR DID YOU FORGET YOUR DEODORANT?!

DROP DEAD, SUSIE! YOU'RE SO UGLY, I HEAR YOUR MOM PUTS A BAG OVER YOUR HEAD BEFORE SHE KISSES YOU GOODNIGHT!!

IT'S SHAMELESS THE WAY WE FLIRT.

WHAT'S IT LIKE TO FALL IN LOVE?

WELL... SAY THE OBJECT OF YOUR AFFECTION WALKS BY...

YEAH?

FIRST, YOUR HEART FALLS INTO YOUR STOMACH AND SPLASHES YOUR INNARDS.

ALL THE MOISTURE MAKES YOU SWEAT PROFUSELY.

THIS CONDENSATION SHORTS THE CIRCUITS TO YOUR BRAIN, AND YOU GET ALL WOOZY.

WHEN YOUR BRAIN BURNS OUT ALTOGETHER, YOUR MOUTH DISENGAGES AND YOU BABBLE LIKE A CRETIN UNTIL SHE LEAVES.

THAT'S LOVE?!?

MEDICALLY SPEAKING.

HECK, THAT HAPPENED TO ME ONCE, BUT I FIGURED IT WAS COOTIES!!

46

Hey, Calvin, it's gonna cost you 50 cents to be my friend today.

AND WHAT IF I DON'T *WANT* TO BE YOUR FRIEND TODAY?

Then the janitor scrapes you off the wall with a spatula.

HECK, WHAT'S A LITTLE EXTORTION AMONG FRIENDS?

I GOT THE NEW ALBUM BY SCRAMBLED DEBUTANTE.

ALL THEIR SONGS GLORIFY DEPRAVED VIOLENCE, MINDLESS SEX, AND THE DELIBERATE ABUSE OF DANGEROUS DRUGS.

YOUR MOM'S GOING TO GO INTO CONNIPTIONS WHEN SHE SEES *THIS* LYING AROUND.

WELL I SURE DIDN'T BUY IT FOR THE MUSIC...

MOM, WILL YOU DRIVE ME INTO TOWN?

WHY SHOULD I *DRIVE* YOU, CALVIN? IT'S A PERFECT DAY OUTSIDE!

WHAT DO YOU THINK PEOPLE HAVE *FEET* FOR?

TO WORK THE GAS PEDAL.

How are you today? Fine.

I want the top of my head shaved, and the sides dyed pink and cut in horizontal stripes, OK?

Ma'am?

Give him the usual, Pete.

Well I guess this guy knows which side HIS bread is buttered on!

There, how's that look?

That's great. Perfect.

Without question, this is the finest haircut I have ever received.

Never criticize a guy with a razor...

61

RISE AND SHINE, CALVIN!

MFGPBTHBBPT

THE EARLY BIRD GETS THE WORM!

BIG INCENTIVE.

I'VE DECIDED WE SHOULD BE "COOLER" THAN WE ARE.

WE'RE NOT COOL?

SURE WE'RE COOL. BUT WE'RE NOT AS COOL AS WE COULD BE.

COOL PEOPLE WEAR DARK GLASSES!

IT'S COOL TO BUMP INTO THINGS?

YOU DON'T MOVE, YOU JUST HANG AROUND.

HEY, DAD, WILL YOU BUY ME A FLAME THROWER?

OF COURSE NOT. DON'T BE SILLY.

EVEN IF I DIDN'T USE IT IN THE HOUSE?

"SAFARI AL" HACKS HIS WAY THROUGH THE JUNGLE!

SUDDENLY, A GIANT GORILLA RIPS THROUGH THE FOLIAGE!

CLEAN YOUR ROOM.

WHAT?

YOU HEARD ME. IT'S A JUNGLE IN HERE!

SEEN ANY UFOs YET?

NOPE.

KEEP WATCHING THE MOON. ALIENS USUALLY TRY TO SNEAK UP FROM BEHIND IT.

WHAT ARE YOU DOING OUT HERE IN YOUR PAJAMAS? GET BACK IN BED!!

MOTHERS, ON THE OTHER HAND, SNEAK UP FROM BEHIND THE PACHYSANDRA PATCH.

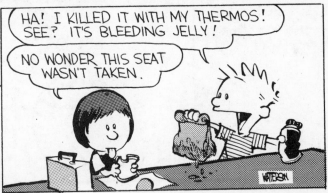

SOMEWHERE IN COMMUNIST RUSSIA I'LL BET THERE'S A LITTLE BOY WHO HAS NEVER KNOWN ANYTHING BUT **CENSORSHIP** AND **OPPRESSION**.

BUT MAYBE HE'S HEARD ABOUT **AMERICA**, AND HE DREAMS OF LIVING IN THIS LAND OF **FREEDOM** AND OPPORTUNITY!

SOMEDAY, I'D LIKE TO MEET THAT LITTLE BOY...

...AND TELL HIM THE AWFUL **TRUTH** ABOUT THIS PLACE!!

CALVIN, BE QUIET AND EAT THE STUPID LIMA BEANS.

WHENEVER I TAKE MY BATH....

...I ALWAYS PUT MY DUCKY IN FIRST.

FOR COMPANIONSHIP?

TO TEST FOR SHARKS.

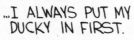

MY SECRET ANCIENT TREASURE MAP SAYS TO DIG HERE!

LOOK! A WALLET FULL OF MONEY! RIGHT WHERE YOU SAID!

IT'S DAD'S. I BURIED IT HERE LAST WEEK.

SPACEMAN SPIFF, BOLD INTERPLANETARY EXPLORER, SPIES A ZARG!

SPIFF CALIBRATES HIS BLASTER. READY...AIM...

CALVIN, IF YOU SHOOT THAT PAPER CLIP AT ME, I'LL GET YOUR BOTTOM HAULED TO THE PRINCIPAL'S OFFICE SO FAST YOU'LL THINK YOU WERE IN A **TIME WARP**!!

CONFOUND IT. THE BLASTER JAMMED.

IT LOOKS LIKE HOBBES BURST A SEAM HERE. I'LL GET MY SEWING KIT.

IT'S JUST A LITTLE CUT. I DON'T NEED AN OPERATION. THIS IS UNNECESSARY SURGERY!

IT'S NOT SURGERY. YOU'RE JUST GETTING A COUPLE STITCHES! WHAT'S THE BIG DEAL?

YOUR MOM NEVER USES ANY ANESTHETIC.

WHAT A PECULIAR DREAM I HAD LAST NIGHT!

I DREAMED I WAS IN A BIG FIGHT WITH A FEROCIOUS WEASEL!

WHAT DO YOU SUPPOSE IT MEANS?

IT MEANS YOU'RE SLEEPING ON THE FLOOR TONIGHT, YOU NINCOMPOOP!

FEARLESS SPACEMAN SPIFF CLOSES IN ON THE FLEEING ZARGONS!

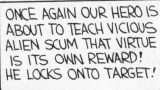

ONCE AGAIN OUR HERO IS ABOUT TO TEACH VICIOUS ALIEN SCUM THAT VIRTUE IS ITS OWN REWARD! HE LOCKS ONTO TARGET!

PSST, CALVIN! WHAT WAS THE CAPITAL OF POLAND UNTIL 1600?

KRAKOW.

THANKS.

KRAKOW! KRAKOW! TWO DIRECT HITS!

THE TYRANNOSAURUS LUMBERS ACROSS THE PREHISTORIC VALLEY...

THE TERRIFYING LIZARD IS THREE STORIES TALL AND HIS MOUTH IS FILLED WITH SIX-INCH CHISELS OF DEATH!

WITH A FEW MIGHTY STEPS, THE DINOSAUR IS UPON A TRIBE OF FLEEING CAVEMEN. HE DEVOURS THEM ONE BY ONE!

AARRGH! AAIEEE! AAUGHH!

CALVIN, EAT YOUR POPCORN QUIETLY!

WHAT DOES THIS WORD MEAN?

WHICH ONE?

THAT LONG ONE.

!

I DON'T KNOW.

YOU DO TOO!! ALL RIGHT! WHERE'S A DICTIONARY??

CALVIN, THE HUMAN INSECT, WALKS ACROSS THE DINNER TABLE.

WITH PROPORTIONAL INSECT STRENGTH, HE PLACES A GIANT PEA ON THE EDGE OF A SPOON.

HE THEN CLIMBS TO THE TOP OF THE OTHER END...

...AND WITH A TINY JUMP...

CALVIN, STOP THAT!

IN HIS MINUSCULE SIZE, IT TAKES CALVIN, THE HUMAN INSECT, TEN MINUTES TO WALK ACROSS A BOOK'S PAGE!

AT THE OTHER END, HE SLOWLY LIFTS THE GIGANTIC SHEET!

THEN IT'S ANOTHER TEN-MINUTE JOURNEY BACK, AS HE TURNS IT OVER!

GEE, THE KID'S BEEN QUIET FOR ALMOST TWENTY MINUTES.

HE'S DOING HIS HOMEWORK.

HERE'S A MOVIE WE SHOULD WATCH.

WHO'S IN IT?

IT SAYS, "JAPANESE CAST."

"TWO BIG RUBBERY MONSTERS SLUG IT OUT OVER MAJOR METROPOLITAN CENTERS IN A BATTLE FOR WORLD SUPREMACY."

DOESN'T THAT SOUND GREAT?

AND PEOPLE SAY THAT FOREIGN FILM IS INACCESSIBLE.

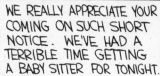
OH, ROSALYN, YOU'RE HERE! GOOD, COME IN!

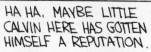
WE REALLY APPRECIATE YOUR COMING ON SUCH SHORT NOTICE. WE'VE HAD A TERRIBLE TIME GETTING A BABY SITTER FOR TONIGHT.

HA HA, MAYBE LITTLE CALVIN HERE HAS GOTTEN HIMSELF A REPUTATION.

HA HA. YOU HAVE THE HALF UP FRONT?

YES, LET ME GET MY PURSE...

HI, BABY DOLL, IT'S ME. YEAH, I'M BABY SITTING THE KID DOWN THE STREET.

YEAH, THAT'S RIGHT, THE LITTLE MONSTER. ...HMM?... WELL SO FAR, NO PROBLEM.

HE HASN'T BEEN ANY TROUBLE. YOU JUST HAVE TO SHOW THESE KIDS WHO'S THE BOSS. ...MM HMM..

HOW MUCH LONGER TILL SHE LETS US OUT OF THE GARAGE?

SHE SAID 8 O'CLOCK, AND IT'S ALMOST 6:30 NOW...

THANKS AGAIN FOR BABY SITTING, ROSALYN.

CALVIN WAS NO TROUBLE AT ALL.

THAT'S GOOD. I'LL GET THE CAR AND DRIVE YOU HOME.

THERE YOU GO. GOOD NIGHT.

THANK YOU. GOOD NIGHT.

IS SHE GONE?

90

MOM! MOM! A BIG DOG KNOCKED ME DOWN AND HE STOLE HOBBES!

I TRIED TO CATCH HIM, BUT I COULDN'T, AND NOW I'VE LOST MY BEST FRIEND!

WELL CALVIN, IF YOU WOULDN'T DRAG THAT TIGER EVERYWHERE, THINGS LIKE THIS WOULDN'T HAPPEN.

THERE'S NO PROBLEM SO AWFUL THAT YOU CAN'T ADD SOME GUILT TO IT AND MAKE IT EVEN WORSE!

I CAN'T SLEEP AT ALL. POOR HOBBES! I WONDER WHERE HE IS. I HOPE HE'S OK.

SNIFF.. WHAT DID I EVER DO TO DESERVE THIS?

WHATEVER IT WAS, I'M *SORRY* ALREADY!

LOST: MY TIGER, "HOBBES"

MAYBE YOU SHOULD DESCRIBE HIM.

ON THE QUIET SIDE. SOMEWHAT PECULIAR. A GOOD COMPANION, IN A WEIRD SORT OF WAY.

I MEAN, WHAT DOES HE LOOK LIKE?

OH.

WELL LOOK, SOMEBODY LEFT A STUFFED TIGER OUT IN THE FIELD. HOW STRANGE.

LOOKS LIKE A DOG'S BEEN CHEWING ON YOU, FELLA.

WELL, NOTHING A LITTLE TEA PARTY WITH SOME OTHER STUFFED ANIMALS WOULDN'T HELP. C'MON.

HOBBES! HOBBES! WHERE ARE YOU??

HELLO, CALVIN. WOULD YOU LIKE TO JOIN MY TEA PARTY?

HECK NO. I'M TRYING TO FIND MY BEST FRIEND, WHO'S BEEN KIDNAPPED BY A DOG. LEAVE ME ALONE.

WELL I THINK MR. CALVIN IS VERY RUDE, DON'T YOU, MR. TIGER? YES, I THINK SO TOO. MORE TEA, ANYONE?

HEY, I SHOULD TELL SUSIE TO KEEP HER EYES OPEN FOR HOBBES.

SUSIE, I... HOBBES!

YOU FOUND HOBBES! THANK YOU THANK YOU THANKYOUTHANKYOUTHANKY OUTHANKYOUTHANKYOUTHA

WELL! WASN'T MR. CALVIN A GENTLEMAN! I DO HOPE... HEY! WHO TOOK ALL THE COOKIES?!?

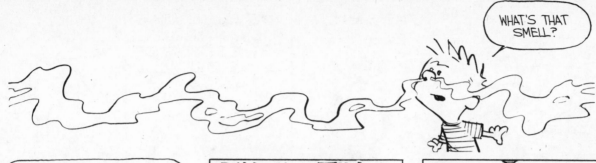

WHAT'S THAT SMELL?

EITHER MOM'S COOKING DINNER, OR SOMEBODY GOT SICK IN THE FURNACE DUCT.

BOY, DOES IT **STINK** IN HERE! WHAT ARE YOU COOKING FOR DINNER?!

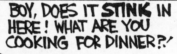

WHATEVER IT IS, I'M NOT EATING IT.

I'M STEWING SOME MONKEY HEADS.

MONKEY HEADS?

THEY'LL BE SOGGY ENOUGH TO EAT IN ABOUT TWENTY MINUTES.

REALLY?? WE'RE HAVING MONKEY HEADS? WE ARE NOT. ...ARE THOSE REALLY MONKEY HEADS?

I'VE NEVER HAD MONKEY HEADS BEFORE! I WONDER WHAT THEY'RE LIKE.

WOW! MONKEY HEADS!

MM...KINDA SQUISHY. OOH LOOK, IS THAT A NOSE? WHAT'S THIS? BRAINS? I DIDN'T THINK THEY'D BE SO RUBBERY...

WHAT? I THOUGHT THESE WERE STUFFED PEPPERS. HONEY, WHAT THE HECK **IS** THIS?? WHATEVER IT IS, I'M NOT EATING IT!

93

SUSIE, WANNA HEAR A SECRET?

SURE.

I THINK THE PRINCIPAL IS A SPACE ALIEN SPY.

HE'S TRYING TO CORRUPT OUR YOUNG INNOCENT MINDS SO WE'LL BE UNABLE TO RESIST WHEN HIS PEOPLE INVADE EARTH!

PROMISE NOT TO TELL ANYONE?

DON'T WORRY.

HOBBES, WHAT SHOULD I DO WHEN MOE COMES TO BEAT ME UP IN GYM CLASS?

WELL, YOU CAN ALWAYS DO WHAT WE TIGERS DO WHEN A RHINO CHARGES.

WHAT'S THAT?

WE SCRAMBLE LIKE MANIACS FOR THE NEAREST TREE.

THAT'S YOUR ADVICE?? TO SIT IN A TREE ALL DAY?!?

IT DOESN'T IMPRESS THE GIRLS, OF COURSE, BUT THERE'S NO SENSE IMPRESSING THEM AND THEN GETTING KILLED, MY DAD USED TO SAY...

HOBBES, I NEED YOUR HELP. THAT BULLY MOE KEEPS PUSHING ME AROUND.

...SO I WANT YOU TO COME TO SCHOOL AND EAT HIM, OK?

EAT HIM?

SURE! TIGERS EAT PEOPLE ALL THE TIME!

WHAT IF THE CAFETERIA LADIES WON'T LET ME USE THE OVEN?

THE WATER'S TOO COLD!

NOW IT'S TOO HOT.

NOW IT'S TOO COLD.

NOW IT'S TOO DEEP.

THE FEARSOME SHARK SENSES DISTRESS IN THE WAVES ABOVE HIM!

HE CIRCLES UP, CLOSER AND CLOSER TO THE TERRIFIED VICTIM!

HEY! YAHH! SNAP THRASH SNAP.

YOU KNOW, FOR SOMEONE WHO HATES BATHS AS MUCH AS YOU DO, YOU'RE NOT MAKING THIS GO ANY FASTER!

ANOTHER GRUESOME KILL...

WHEN ARE WE GOING TO GET TO OUR VACATION SITE? I WANNA *BE* THERE!

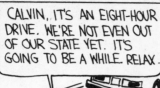

CALVIN, IT'S AN EIGHT-HOUR DRIVE. WE'RE NOT EVEN OUT OF OUR STATE YET. IT'S GOING TO BE A WHILE. RELAX.

HOW MUCH LONGER *NOW*?

I TOLD YOU WE SHOULD HAVE FLOWN.

THERE'S A RESTAURANT COMING UP. WANT TO STOP?

ONLY IF THEY HAVE HAMBURGERS.

HAMBURGERS? THAT'S ALL WE'VE EATEN THIS WHOLE STUPID TRIP! HAMBURGERS, HAMBURGERS, HAMBURGERS!

I'M SICK OF HAMBURGERS! WE'RE EATING SOMETHING ELSE FOR ONCE!

TEN MILLION BOTTLES OF BEER ON THE WALL, TEN MILLION BOTTLES OF BEER...

OK! OK! HERE'S A HAMBURGER JOINT! *ARE YOU HAPPY?!*

I HAVE TO GO TO THE BATHROOM.

CALVIN, WE JUST PULLED OUT OF THE RESTAURANT. CAN'T YOU WAIT? THINK OF SOMETHING ELSE.

ALL I CAN THINK OF IS NIAGARA FALLS, AND THE HOOVER DAM, AND NOAH'S ARK, AND...

OOH BOY, NOW *I* HAVE TO GO!

NEXT YEAR I SWEAR I'LL JUST TAKE A VACATION BY MYSELF.

THAT TRIP WAS EXCRUCIATING. THANK GOODNESS WE'RE HERE.

EIGHT HOURS CRAMMED IN A CAR WITH A HYPERACTIVE SIX-YEAR-OLD! WHAT AN ORDEAL!

WELL, NOW CALVIN CAN RUN AND SCREAM ALL HE LIKES. AHH, WHAT A GREAT LITTLE PLACE.

I'M BORED. WHEN ARE WE LEAVING?

YOU'RE BORED? WOULD YOU LIKE ME TO SHOW YOU HOW AN ANCHOR WORKS?

AHH! ANOTHER GLORIOUS SUNRISE, AND NOT A SOUL AROUND!

THIS IS THE LIFE! A BRISK SWIM AT DAWN, A MORNING OUT IN A BOAT...

...AND BY 9 A.M., I'M BACK WITH FRESHLY CAUGHT FISH FOR BREAKFAST! THE DAY'S HARDLY BEGUN! WHAT A VACATION!

UGH...I'VE SEEN CHEERIER FACES AT THE OFFICE!

YOU EAT YOUR DEAD ANIMALS. ALL I WANT IS SOME COFFEE.

WHY ISN'T THERE ANY TV UP HERE? I HATE THIS PLACE.

DAD, LOOK! I CAUGHT A FISH!

HEY, THAT'S A BIG ONE. I'LL SHOW YOU HOW TO CLEAN IT, AND WE'LL HAVE IT FOR DINNER.

"CLEAN IT"?

CUT OFF ITS HEAD AND GUT IT.

MMM! PASS ME ANOTHER OF THESE GREAT CHEESE SANDWICHES! HA HA, NO BONES IN THESE, RIGHT?

IT'S ANOTHER NEW MORNING FOR MR. MONROE. HE GLANCES AT THE NEWSPAPER HEADLINES OVER A CUP OF COFFEE, AND GETS IN HIS RED SPORTS CAR TO GO TO WORK.

LITTLE DOES HE REALIZE IT'S HIS LAST DAY ON THE FACE OF THE EARTH!

CALVIN DRINKS THE MAGIC ELIXIR AND BEGINS AN INCREDIBLE TRANSFORMATION!

INSTANTLY HE GROWS! BIGGER AND BIGGER! HIGHER AND HIGHER!

HE IS NOW OVER 300 FEET TALL! THE FORMULA IS A SUCCESS!

CALVIN, THE MIGHTY GIANT, GOES ON A TERRIBLE RAMPAGE, STRIKING FEAR INTO THE HEARTS OF THE POPULACE!

NOTHING CAN STOP HIM! IT'S PANIC IN THE STREETS! A TOWN LIES IN RUINS!

NO, I WON'T BUY YOU ANY MORE TOY CARS. I SAW YOU! YOU DELIBERATELY STOMPED ON THOSE!

119

Calvin: LOOK AT THAT THING IN THE DIRT! IT MUST BE A FOSSIL!

Calvin: I WONDER WHAT PECULIAR ANIMAL *THIS* WAS.

Calvin: BUT IT'S NOT A BONE. IT MUST BE SOME PRIMITIVE HUNTING WEAPON OR EATING UTENSIL FOR CAVE MEN.

Hobbes: MAYBE IT HAD SOME RELIGIOUS FUNCTION.

THIS EXPLAINS WHY YOUR CLOTHES STAY ON THE FLOOR.

Hobbes: MAKING A SIGN?

Calvin: I'M DECLARING THE CREEK BACK IN THE WOODS "CALVIN'S CREEK."

Calvin: WHEN YOU DISCOVER SOMETHING, YOU'RE ALLOWED TO NAME IT AND PUT UP A SIGN.

Calvin's Creek

Hobbes: BUT SUPPOSE YOU DIDN'T DISCOVER THAT CREEK.

Calvin: OF COURSE I DID! NOBODY *ELSE* HAS A SIGN THERE, RIGHT?

Hobs Crk

Calvin: CAN HOBBES AND I GO PLAY IN THE RAIN, MOM?

Mom: NO.

Calvin: WHY NOT?

Mom: YOU'LL GET SOAKED.

Calvin: WHAT'S WRONG WITH THAT?

Mom: YOU COULD CATCH PNEUMONIA, RUN UP A TERRIBLE HOSPITAL BILL, LINGER A FEW MONTHS, AND DIE.

Calvin: I ALWAYS FORGET. IF YOU ASK A MOM, YOU GET A WORST-CASE SCENARIO.

Hobbes: I HAD NO IDEA THESE LITTLE SHOWERS WERE SO *DANGEROUS*.

WANT TO GO SPELUNKING WITH ME?

SPELUNKING? THERE AREN'T ANY CAVES AROUND HERE!

YOU DON'T NEED A CAVE. ALL YOU NEED IS A ROCK.

SPELUNK!

WELL DAD, OFF TO WORK?

TOO BAD. *I'M* ON SUMMER VACATION, SO *I* GET TO STAY HOME AND DO WHATEVER I WANT.

WELL, GO OFF AND JOIN THE RAT RACE! MOM AND I ARE RACKING UP LOTS OF EXPENSES!

OOG.

I JUST DO THAT TO HELP HIM APPRECIATE THE WEEKENDS MORE.

HOT DAY, ISN'T IT?

I'LL SAY.

BUT IT'S THE HUMIDITY THAT REALLY GETS TO ME.

YOU DON'T LIKE IT WHEN IT'S HUMID?

NOT AT ALL.

THEN YOU'D BETTER GET OUT QUICK.

124

Finis